'H[...] rears
and to channel our energy into what we can be hopeful for. Katie
Piper is a symbol of hope wh[...]gs can
get better, no matter how [...]inds us
to have faith.'
Kamran Bedi, life coach an[...]

'Katie is THE example of a po[...]ve, uplifting human being. Her daily
affirmations on social media are always so encouraging, so to have
them all in one book is such a great idea and will help so many.'
Olivia Bowen, TV personality

'Katie Piper is a sheer force for good, embodying great strength,
resilience, determination and hope. Katie has unflinchingly shared
her experiences and the life lessons she's garnered over the years
with her million-strong community, helping them to feel inspired and
empowered. Her wise and nourishing daily mantras within this book
will provide you too with the courage to transform your life, and it
couldn't come at a more poignant or apt time.'
**Vicki Broadbent, founder of HonestMum.com, bestselling author
of *Mumboss* and TV broadcaster**

'Katie Piper is such an empowering person. Anyone who has strug-
gled with adversity and fought their way out of tough situations can
take comfort and inspiration from her approach to life.'
Matt Haig, author

'Katie embodies strength, resilience and positivity, and that is truly
reflected in her new book. If you're in need of something to lift you
up and fill you with confidence, then this book is for you.'
Alice Liveing, personal trainer, author and Instagrammer

'Katie is such a shining light and positive role model for so many, including me. This book will uplift readers with her advice, positivity and spirituality.'
Andrea McLean, TV presenter and *Sunday Times* bestselling author

'Katie personifies all the traits I most admire in people: courage, resilience, determination, mental strength, a refusal to do self-pity, and a fantastically positive and optimistic view of life whatever hurdles are put in her way.'
Piers Morgan, broadcaster, journalist, writer and television personality

'A wonderful and uplifting book for those who need daily guidance and light in their lives.'
Louise Pentland, author, YouTuber and UN ambassador

'In a world that often feels designed to prevent recovery from trauma, Katie Piper is the inspirational warrior we all need. A champion of how to survive and then thrive no matter what tragedy life sends our way, Katie Piper is someone we admire greatly, and we often look to her for positive words and affirmations to pick us up.'
Ian Redpath and Jeremy Chopra, authors of *All on the Board*

'Katie's zest for life is a tonic for the soul.'
Susanna Reid, TV presenter

'Katie personifies heart, courage, endurance and hope as the extraordinary woman she is. It is beautifully expressed in this gift of a book that every one of us can learn and grow from.'
Julia Samuel, bestselling author, speaker and psychotherapist

'Faith, positivity and spirituality can be such powerful tools in life. No one epitomizes this more than Katie Piper does.'
Nadia Sawalha, TV presenter and personality

'Katie is one of the most uplifting souls I've come across – online and offline. One minute in her company and you feel anchored by her beautiful rawness and extraordinary energy . . . It's like having a friend in a book.'
Anna Whitehouse, aka Mother Pukka – author, radio presenter and campaigner

'Katie radiates positivity! A book for those who need daily uplifting affirmations from one of the most inspiring women I know. A must-read to brighten up your days.'
Laura Whitmore, author and presenter

'Katie has always been an inspiration to me. She is beautiful inside and out, and has devoted her life to helping and inspiring others, which shows how selfless and amazing she is. Her positivity shines through and her book is the perfect example of this.'
Jessica Wright, TV personality and businesswoman

Katie Piper OBE is a bestselling author, TV presenter and philanthropist.

Described as an 'icon of her generation', Katie secured her place in the nation's hearts when she appeared on Channel 4's BAFTA-nominated documentary *Katie: My Beautiful Face*, which covered the early stages of her recovery after an acid attack in 2008. For over a decade, Katie has devoted her life to the Katie Piper Foundation to support those living with burns and scars; she has received numerous awards, accolades and doctorates for her work.

Katie is a much-loved presenter for the BBC's *Songs of Praise* and BBC Radio 2, the host of the acclaimed *Katie Piper's Extraordinary People* podcast, a panellist on *Loose Women* and the face of iconic global beauty brands. Katie is dedicated to challenging the concept of traditional beauty across the media and will continue to lead thought-promoting diversity, inclusion and acceptance across society.

KATIE PIPER

A Little Bit of Hope

100 Affirmations for Positive Living

First published in Great Britain in 2022

Society for Promoting Christian Knowledge
36 Causton Street
London SW1P 4ST
www.spck.org.uk

British Library Cataloguing-in-Publication Data
A catalogue record for this book is available from the British Library

ISBN 978–0–281–08747–1
eBook ISBN 978–0–281–08746–4

Typeset by Fakenham Prepress Solutions, Fakenham, Norfolk, NR21 8NL
Printed & bound in Great Britain by Clays Ltd, Elcograf S.p.A.

eBook by Fakenham Prepress Solutions, Fakenham, Norfolk, NR21 8NL

Produced on paper from sustainable forests

I dedicate this book to everyone who has had to tap into the power of positive thinking when it felt like the only thing they had left; to the people who have contacted me online, written to me and stopped me in the street or at a restaurant to tell me their story.

We all have our scars to bear, visible or invisible. It's what links us.

You know who you are. This one's for you.

Introduction

Affirmations have been a part of my life for as long as I remember. And yet, after the attack that changed my life for ever, they took on a whole new role in my recovery. The words we speak over ourselves and to each other matter. If we constantly tell ourselves that we can't do something, that we must not step out, that we're not good enough so why even bother, then the chances are we're not going to feel empowered to be the best that we can be.

I, for one, have found reading, meditating, and sharing positive affirmations a game-changer in my attitude and in my life. It's for this reason that I found myself turning back to my favourite phrases and words of wisdom during the global pandemic, sharing these encouragements in my social media stories. Pretty soon, an entire online community of people would connect over hearing, receiving and passing on the same affirmations. In fact, these positive nuggets proved so popular that they formed the basis of my last book, *A Little Bit of Faith – Hopeful affirmations for every day of the year.*

Unlike some of the toxic positivity we can encounter in our culture today, my hope was that these affirmations would feel real, help people engage with *all* their emotions and know that it's OK to not always feel OK. We're all on a journey. The reality is we all have good days and bad days. Even in the weeks since receiving my OBE for my services to charity for the work of the Katie Piper Foundation in helping the victims of burns and scars, I've had days of feeling proud and successful and other days of lacking motivation and feeling the pressure to 'keep up' with the lives of others. One of the things that always keeps me going on these days is remembering who I do a lot of my work for: those whom society can too often overlook or discount.

Accessibility lies at the heart of everything I do. It is for this reason that I felt the need to bring out this new book of affirmations, selecting 100 of my favourites from *A Little Bit of Faith* to enable more people to engage with these encouragements in a shorter, cheaper paperback book that you can take with you wherever you go. I also wanted to help a certain community that is close to my heart . . .

When the initial story about my attack went viral, I was inundated with messages and letters of support from a wide variety of people. Old-school handwritten letters began to fill the post-box at my charity office, but something was different about some of the envelopes – they carried an HMP stamp on them. The first time I received a letter brandishing the sign for Her Majesty's Prison, it gave me heart palpitations and a hot sweat prickled across the back of my neck, but what was inside surprised me: it was a letter from someone just like me; someone who had made decisions that had changed the course of their life for ever; someone who needed support and, like me, wanted a second chance at life.

Male and female prisoners wrote, sharing stories with me of growing up around or as a victim of domestic violence that had left them feeling broken and rejected by society. I felt a deep empathy and duty and, knowing how much time, effort and even expense it would have taken to contact me, I wrote back to everyone. I know regret, loss of identity and purpose, and I also believe in rehabilitation. As my rehabilitation progressed in the outside world, I began volunteering inside prisons and also made a documentary with Channel 4 with male offenders, helping them to prepare for release. A unit in a women's prison has now been named after me and I continue to work in prisons and refuge houses, always learning more from the clients than I feel I have to share with them. It is a true honour.

The truth is, more than three in five people in prison are assessed as having poor literary skills, which means reading the newspaper or a household bill can be hard work – never mind reading a book. It is for this reason that I have specifically designed these affirmations to be in short bite-size chunks that you can dip in and out of. It is also why I have decided to make a donation for every copy of *A Little Bit of Hope* sold to support Diffusion Books, a charitable arm of my publisher SPCK, which produces fiction books for use in prisons that are age-appropriate for adult readers but are designed for those with a lower literacy level. There is clear evidence that improving prisoners' reading skills has a huge impact on their prospects for effective rehabilitation and reintegration to society. Not only that, but each of the books created by Diffusion Books carries a moral story and questions for reflection at the end of each chapter. It is for this reason that I have decided to end each affirmation in this book with a question to help you put every affirmation into action in your life.

Whether you are a prisoner, a teenager, a busy person reading these affirmations before work or a stressed parent trying to sleep better by reflecting in the evening, my hope is that these simple affirmations will leave you feeling more hope-filled today and hopeful for tomorrow.

Love,

Katie x

Nothing can stop you from letting go and making a fresh start.

I'm not sure where you're at in your journey right now but making a fresh start can often seem far from simple. When I see barriers in my path, I like to ask myself, 'Who put them there?' Through my own self-development and working with others over the years, I've found that the barriers we feel restricted by are often those we put in place ourselves. Have you created a barrier that's stopping you from being victorious? Do you need to reframe it to empower yourself to see your 'fresh start' as a possibility?

I will repeat things that I need to hear.

I am well aware that a lot of the messages in this book may be familiar to you already! I find, when I read affirmations, they're often ideas that I already know about, or I've seen on social media before. That doesn't matter. The repetition and saying them out loud means that they sink in a little bit further. Don't be afraid to repeat things over and over. I've found it so helpful in my journey to keep coming back to my favourite affirmations, just as a reminder! Which words do you need to repeat over yourself today?

My scars show strength, not weakness.

Whether you think of physical or mental scars when you read this, it's still true. I know that the scars we carry tell a story of what we've lived through, what we've survived and the strength we have coming out the other side. Don't hide your scars; wear them with pride! Is there a 'scar' you need to challenge yourself to share with someone else?

Day 4

I will challenge myself.

Some of the affirmations in this book will suggest a way forward or a change of mindset, but sometimes I think that a good affirmation leads us instead to think more deeply about something and come to our own conclusions. While you work through these 100 days of affirmations, remember to ask yourself the question: 'Are there any affirmations I have already read that I could go back to and challenge myself to think about in more depth?' You have the power to challenge yourself and change. We are often more courageous than we first think. As you journey through this book, ask yourself: 'Is there anything I'm brushing over because it feels too hard?' Can you mark out some time to look over it afresh?

You don't have to see the whole staircase, just take the first step.

Martin Luther King Jr

(M. Marable and L. Mullings (eds), *Let Nobody Turn Us Around*, Rowman & Littlefield, 2003)

I know that when you're anxious, doing anything without a guaranteed outcome is a huge challenge. We all want to know how the journey will end when we set out. I understand that I'm never going to know the story from start to finish so, for me, I draw on my faith to keep me going. Believing that I'm being looked out for, and that there is a plan for my life, means I don't feel so scared when I take that first step. Is there a step forward that you could take today but have been putting off because you don't know what the outcome will be?

Day 6

I will recognize and embrace all the emotions that I was designed to feel.

It's important to allow yourself to experience your feelings. It can sometimes feel as if today's culture is rife with toxic positivity and the need to put a positive spin on whatever we are going through, but our emotions are a positive thing and we shouldn't be afraid to feel them. Even now, I have some days where I feel happy and successful and others where I feel I'm missing the mark. Tears can be a physical release of built-up tension. Don't suppress the force of your emotions. Is there a particular emotion that keeps bubbling up for you this week? Take some time out and allow yourself to feel and explore the root of this emotion properly.

Life is too short to be spent at war with yourself.

In an ideal world, we would be our own ally, cheerleader and friend. In real life, though, I know that I can be my harshest critic and worst companion! Far from being nasty to those around us, we can hold the biggest grudges against ourselves. In the end, who is that anger helping? Definitely not us. Is there something that you could forgive yourself for today?

It is in the darkest skies that stars are best seen.

Richard Paul Evans

(*Timepiece*, Pocket Books, 1997)

It's when the toughest times have hit in my life, or during my darkest nights, that I've found my greatest strength. They've also helped me to see the people I can truly rely on more clearly. It's those bright stars – the people, my passions – that help me get through. If you're suffering it's horrific, but maybe in the future you'll see a new meaning in that terrible time. Where can you see glimmers of brightness breaking through your dark night?

Love looks outwards.

Some people might think affirmations are self-centred or all about ourselves, but in reality I have found that reminding myself to have an outward-minded attitude and perspective has always been far more rewarding for me than looking inwards – and the affirmations in this book will continue to encourage us to look 'out' as well as 'in'.

I think the ultimate expression of love is putting the needs of someone else before my own. It also helps me not to be so focused on my own troubles, needs and successes but, instead, to see the world as a community where, ultimately, we're working towards a common good. How can you look outwards today?

I will just 'get on with it'.

When I was at my lowest point, my mum was quite funny. I remember crying to her one day and she simply said, 'Well, you're just going to have to get on with it, dear!' It's become a family in-joke that we say to each other when someone has a mountain to climb. It's not always a good idea to be so straight-talking with people, but sometimes bluntness is just what you need! Do you need to do some straight talking to yourself or your circumstances today?

I can stay positive when others are negative.

This is definitely an affirmation that you have to vocalize! I have to say this out loud repeatedly until I actually start to believe it. When people around you are down or anxious or angry, fighting the urge to join them isn't easy. I have to tell myself not to get sucked in. Is there a situation in your life right now where you might just be following the crowd? How can you stand out among them?

There is wonder in everybody, and I will choose to look for it.

Look for the best in each person you meet, and you will find it. I'm always blown away by the stories people have to share and the things that they've been through. There really is something miraculous and inspiring and incredible in each person's life. Who could you challenge yourself to take the time to listen to and connect with today in order to uncover some gold?

I don't have to relate to every motivational quote.

I've found that positive quotes can rile me up if they're not well-thought-through. What good does it do, telling someone to get up and run with the sunshine on their face, if they've been in an accident and are unable to walk? Not everyone has the option to 'seize the day'. If that's where you're at, then that's OK. Know that regardless of how some 'positive' messages can make you feel, you're doing your best and your best is more than enough. And, if you feel riled up (as I sometimes do), remember you can use this passion for a purpose. How can you ensure tone-deaf messages are counteracted in the way you communicate today?

To cure jealousy is to see it for what it is: a dissatisfaction with self.

Joan Didion

I've realized that a lot of negative emotions are more about ourselves than the person they're directed towards. Don't feel ashamed, though – we can all fall into a trap of feeling jealous. I know I have from time to time! The best thing we can do is ask ourselves why we're feeling that way – is it telling us that we would like to make a change in our own lives?

I will give my mind permission to take a break.

I am a big fan of locking my office door for the weekend, partly so the kids don't get in and mess it up, but also so I won't be tempted to sneak in and work. It's a relief to turn the key in the lock and say to myself, 'Whatever hasn't been finished, I'm not going to let it seep into my weekend.' That boundary is important for me but it can be hard for those who don't have the luxury of physically moving from one space to another. Even so, I think it's important that we draw a line under our work or our worries. Could you give yourself a cut-off point for worrying or trying to mentally work out a problem and turn your mind to something else instead?

I will think of solutions.

I know this isn't always the right thing to say, and pushing ourselves to 'fix' things is sometimes damaging, but there are times when we're so focused on the problem that we don't see the solution. Other times, I think that the solution could be right in front of us but we don't see it because it doesn't look how we thought it would. Could you turn your attention to solutions today?

I don't know what's round the corner and I choose to let that excite me rather than scare me.

The mystery of what's coming next is both one of the best and one of the worst things about life. I choose to see the unknown as a place of opportunity and I am excited to see what's waiting for me. Taking this approach can be really tough, though, particularly if you've experienced some real pain or trauma in your past. All the same, I like to allow myself to open up to the idea that better things are on the horizon and be excited about them! Can you challenge yourself to read this affirmation every time uncertainty about the future begins to rob you of your joy?

A family doesn't have to be perfect, it just has to be united.

All relationships are complicated. People aren't perfect – I know I'm not! So forgiveness is key, because we will all make mistakes in life. Maintaining unity, even when someone has upset you, is a way of showing that person you have their back, no matter what, and we all need that. Who can you extend forgiveness to today?

Day 19

I will say sorry when I'm wrong.

Apologies are powerful. I know that I can find it hard to say sorry when I'm wrong, particularly with the people I'm closest to! Far from admitting weakness, saying sorry shows huge strength. It takes humility to recognize your own part in a situation, back down and make amends. I've always thought that people who apologize well show great character.

Could you be that person today?

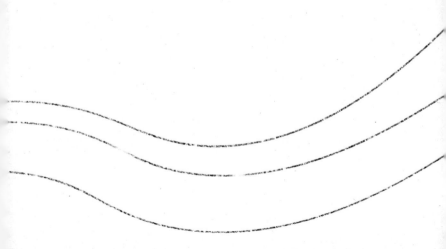

Surround yourself with people who are willing to elevate and celebrate you.

It's our personal responsibility to make sure we surround ourselves with positive things. That includes the people in our lives and if we're on social media, the people in our 'feeds' and 'timelines'. We always talk about social media as if it's this horrible beast, but there's so much good in it too. It's given a voice to the voiceless and I love using social media to provide a platform for things that matter, for example my series of #MindsetMonday posts on Instagram that seeks to celebrate people who are overcoming great adversity and inspiring others. What influence and information are you surrounding yourself with? Is it having a positive impact on you?

I will stand up
and speak up for my rights.

We all have fundamental rights – or, at least, we should do. Injustice is all around us on this Earth. Unfortunately, it's often the least, the last and the lost – those who don't have a strong voice – who suffer most. That means if you don't fall into that category, maybe you can do something to stand up for someone else who doesn't have the chance for their voice to be heard. When the strongest stand up and shout loudly on behalf of others, those who are weaker gain their strength. So who can you stand up for today?

You are not your mistakes; they are what you did, not who you are.

Lisa Lieberman-Wang

I truly believe in rehabilitation, and thank Lisa very much for giving me permission to quote her wise words here. I believe everyone should have the chance to do things better next time. From the small mishaps all the way to those people coming out of prison, I hate the idea of condemning someone or writing them off as a lost cause when, really, who you are and your mistakes are two different things. We've all done things in the past that we don't associate with who we are now and we all need another chance. Do you need to separate yourself from a particular past mistake today?

I can't be strong all the time and that's OK.

Not all difficult situations have a clear-cut or one solution. Sometimes the best thing you can do in the face of trials is to allow yourself to feel what you feel. I love a good cry from time to time – it's therapeutic! Allowing yourself to experience your emotions, instead of dumbing them down or trying to mask them, is a really healthy thing to do. Feeling something is being strong! Are there any pent-up emotions you need to find a healthy way to release?

Day 24

I will not chase short-term fixes to long-term problems.

We can all look for comfort in the wrong places. Goodness knows, I've tried all kinds of ways to patch things up in the past! I've now learnt that embracing and acknowledging hardship will mean that I move through it so much faster than I would if I gave in to a seemingly quick fix. Don't distract yourself from difficult things. No situation will actually be made better by alcohol, drugs, sex, betting, overeating or any other damaging coping mechanism. How can you sit with your feelings today?

I will not play it small when I was made to live life in all its fullness.

The options we have in life are so endless. I think I really started living life to its fullest when I found my passion for and my purpose in what I do, a large part of which is the work we are doing with the survivors of burns and scars through the Katie Piper Foundation. This discovery also came with risk. I had to run the risk that I would fail. Every time I put myself out there to try to achieve my dreams, I faced the possibility of rejection. That's tough, but when it's in service of your passion, every part of it feels worth it. Do you know what your passions are? What space might you be able to make for them in this season?

I will not let the disappointments of today keep me from pursuing my dream tomorrow.

It would be such a shame to let something upsetting ruin how you feel about your future. Even if something difficult hits, you're still you. You still have your hopes, dreams and aspirations. To carry the doubts and disappointments of yesterday into today is really giving power or control to the person or issue that caused them. What can you leave behind today?

To exist is to change, to change is to mature, to mature is to go on creating oneself endlessly.

Henri Bergson

(A. Mitchell, C. Brereton, E. E. Slosson and F. L. Pogson (trans.),
The Essential Works of Henri Bergson, e-artnow, 2018)

This is a powerful affirmation, but I see it almost like a beautiful poem too. I think we all need to be reminded of this from time to time; that life will change, and we need to roll with it. Far from being a bad thing, the creative opportunities offered as life changes and we mature are endless. It also reminds me that maturity isn't about age; it's about mindset and experiences. What is one change taking place in your life right now? What opportunities and open doors is it presenting you with?

I will speak kindly and respectfully to myself.

There's a really good exercise someone once told me about that I use all the time. Picture your friend coming to you with a particular problem. Now write out what you would say to your friend. What would you write? It would be compassionate and kind, highlighting your friend's strengths. That's exactly how you should speak to yourself when you have a problem to tackle. Don't put yourself down, but treat yourself with the same love and compassion that you would give your friend. Seeing the words you would use written out is such a powerful exercise. What do you need to say to 'your friend' today?

I will do my bit to make the world a better place.

Sometimes I feel that everyone is trying to build the best lives for themselves alone. The more I think about it, though, the more I feel doing that is a waste of time. If we focus outwards instead, on developing a kind world with a culture of understanding that upholds human dignity, we will all have a better place to live and all our lives will be greatly improved as a result. How can you 'look outwards' this week? What prompts can you put in place to remind you to 'look out'?

Day 30

I will not take a 'no' as a personal attack.

Any time I receive some form of rejection, I ask myself what the 'no' could mean. It could mean the timing's wrong, that the other person isn't ready for what I'm offering or already has something similar in the pipeline. A 'no' is rarely a reflection on you, so you shouldn't take it that way. Write down a recent 'no' you have received from someone and then come up with as many reasons (that have nothing to do with you) for this 'no' as you can. Does it help you depersonalize the rejection?

I will take time for myself today: to pause, to pray, to meditate.

What it means to 'pray' and 'meditate' may take many different forms, depending on what you believe. It may be a moment of quiet reflection before your day. For me, I pray, but I don't pray in the traditional way, with my hands together or on my knees. I often pray in my head while walking around or running errands. Sometimes I say things out loud, as if I'm chatting to a mate. I write little notes and scribble in my journal. These things are valuable for your mind, whether you have a faith or not. I believe that everyone benefits from the sense of off-loading and feeling the peace and calm that come with meditation. Can you try it in your own way today?

I will not compare my life to other people's curated output.

With some people, the only insight you get into their lives is what they show you on social media or in a brief moment of their day. I don't know if you find this, but I can start to build up an impression of them in my own mind that is actually just an edit or a glimpse of a particular version of them.

It's important to remember that we don't know what is going on for someone behind closed doors. Can you recognize when you find yourself comparing your whole life to what someone else is choosing to share with you?

I will learn to trust.

Putting our trust in something can make us feel really vulnerable because we leave ourselves open to being let down. Honestly, though, I have learnt how much better I feel when I trust in something bigger than myself. For me, this is God, but for you it might be something else. In my life, I realize that God doesn't always answer every prayer instantly and there's a lot of suffering in the world, but I believe that trusting in God means letting go and feeling supported for the long run. That's a nice feeling of comfort for me, knowing that trusting can be the safest place of all. Have you had times when someone has broken your trust? What steps might you be able to take to move forward from it today?

I will not judge others based on the small window of their life that I looked through.

Developing empathy is so important for us; for our own mental health, but also for the benefit of those around us and how we treat them. From all my research, I know that often negative behaviours are far more complex than they seem if we take them at face value. If someone hasn't behaved well, why not give them the benefit of the doubt? You don't know what has happened to cause them to act that way. Write down an incident in which you judged someone for their actions or behaviour. What other ways could you choose to look at this?

Never stop doing your best because someone doesn't give you credit.

It is so annoying when someone doesn't credit you for your idea or achievement. The driving force behind what we do, though, shouldn't be the recognition we think that it will get us. When I'm feeling that I should receive more praise, I have to step back and ask myself what my motive was when I started.

Often the answer isn't that I wanted the credit but that I wanted to achieve something or help out. Is there an area in your life where you feel you should get more credit? What was the motive for entering into that project in the first place?

Be grateful when things are going your way; be graceful when they're not.

When things are going great in our lives, we graciously practise gratitude and we allow ourselves to feel it as a privilege. When they're not going so well, though, I've found it's very important to practise dignity. I say 'practise' because it is a skill that we all need to practise, and it doesn't come easily! How could you practise grace for yourself and for others today?

I will keep things in perspective.

I find it helpful to look at problems for what they really are and not what I've built them up to be in my head. I know this technique isn't for everyone, but I break a situation down and ask myself what the worst outcome would be for each scenario. I find that this gives me a better perspective on the situation and reminds me what's important. Can you take the same 'break it down' approach to something you are facing this week?

The hardest thing about 'everything happens for a reason' is waiting for that reason to show up.

Attributed to Karen Salmansohn

I'm not a fan of the saying 'everything happens for a reason' on its own. I find the affirmation above far more realistic. On my own journey, I've found that it's easier to understand experiences with hindsight, and it's often when we look back that we can make sense out of them. With that in mind, if you're waiting to make sense of something now, I want you to find this hopeful. There is a struggle, and you may not understand it now, but you will in time. Can you point to another situation in your life that didn't make sense at the time but with the gift of hindsight you now see more clearly?

I will listen to my body.

Sometimes low self-esteem or, in its more extreme form, self-hatred, can stop us from tuning in to ourselves and our bodies. By observing ourselves, listening to how we're feeling, we can work out what will nourish our minds, souls and physical bodies, which will mean that we can look after ourselves much more effectively. What is your body saying today?

I will get up. I've not lost everything while I still have my life.

If simply getting up each day feels like a struggle, I'm sorry that is the case for you right now. Sadly, you are not alone in this – a number of other people will also relate to needing to speak these words over themselves. I know how it feels to be low and worried about what you've got left in your life. Even if you don't feel it today, know that there is hope for you. There is plenty in your life to make it worth getting up and dusting yourself off again. You can do this! Why not scribble down three things you are thankful for now?

Day 41

I will listen and not interrupt.

Listening sounds like the easiest thing in the world. It involves just sitting there and not saying anything, doesn't it? In reality, it's not that at all! Listening isn't passive; it's an active thing and it's really hard work. It's tough not to interrupt or give your opinion, particularly when you disagree, but sometimes the best gift you can offer someone is a listening ear.

Who can you truly hear today?

I will let go of the life I expected to have and start living the life I was given.

At some point, you've just got to give in and accept where you are. I know, for me, my twenties didn't turn out how I planned them at all. My life was flipped completely upside down, but the longer I resisted that fact, the slower my recovery was. The moment I practised acceptance was the moment things changed. It freed up my head space to focus on getting better and made life so much easier. Is there something you need to learn to accept in your life? Is there a trusted friend or companion you can invite on this journey?

I will not play it safe.

Playing it safe seems like a good idea, but it offers people a false sense of security. Ultimately, everything we do involves a level of risk – even just popping to the shops for a loaf of bread or crossing the road or heading to work! We may as well take those risks, chasing things that we love and actually want. Even if something doesn't go how we'd like, at least we'll know that we tried. What is one area you might need to stop playing it safe in today?

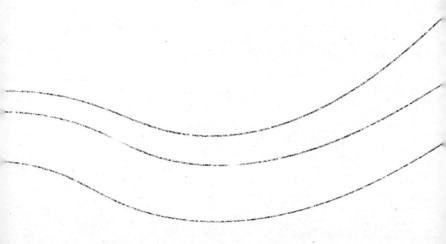

I will not pretend to be something I'm not.

I've found so much freedom in doing this. I know that I am loved by my friends, family and God, and through that I've learnt to love myself. I don't need to hide who I am from anyone. Do you find yourself pretending to be something you're not in order to be liked? Maybe it's time to stop pretending and embrace the real you!

No one can make you feel inferior without your consent.

Eleanor Roosevelt

(*Reader's Digest*, September 1940, Vol. 37, p. 84)

When it comes to other people's words, we can't control what they say, but we can control what we accept. It is hard to stop things having an impact, but if you can be robust and stick to what you know to be true, it makes all the difference. What is most important is what you think of yourself and how proud you are of your own actions, not what someone else says. What do you think about yourself on your best days? Try to remember you're still the same you.

One loyal friend is worth more than a thousand fake ones.

I'm pretty sure social media has trained us to think that the most popular people are the ones with the largest number of 'friends', but, in fact, very few of those 'friendships' will have any real depth or add any value to the person's life. Rather than worrying about accumulating 'friends', I've found that it's more important to invest in and cultivate a few really amazing friendships. Can you list a handful of friends or people in your life whom you genuinely want to invest in?

Sometimes you have to let go of the past with acceptance, value the present with gratitude and anticipate the future with hope.

I don't know about you but, for me, letting go has been a challenge at times. I push myself to do it but it's not always easy. When we do allow ourselves to release our grasp on the past, it frees up our head space to truly enjoy what we have in the present and cultivate hope for the future. What one thing could you let go of or appreciate or look forward to today?

I will remember that no one's life is perfect, even if it seems that way.

It's so easy to look at what someone else has and wish we had it for ourselves, but the reality is never what it seems. Of course, I don't want to picture all the terrible things that could be going on behind the scenes but, in my experience, it's important to remember that you don't know the full extent of someone else's situation. If, however, someone is as successful and happy as they appear, why not feel pleased for them? Troubles come for all of us so they should be allowed to celebrate this time of success! Whose success can you celebrate today?

Not every situation needs a reaction. Some things are better left alone.

I reserve my energy for the people who I know are open to feedback and those I want to continue to grow a relationship with. If you're around someone and you don't particularly want to deepen your connection, why bother correcting them if they do something wrong? It will only cost you to challenge them and what would it achieve? You can't educate everyone. Instead, why not concentrate on the people you care about most?

Comparison is the fastest way to feel unhappy.

I know many people think that comparison arrived with the advent of social media, but I for one remember it being around long before that! I can remember my friends and I comparing our looks or skin or body sizes ages ago. The fact is, even if we all read the same things and used the same creams and ate the same food and exercised the same amount, we'd all end up looking totally different from one another. We're not in competition with others, and seeking to be is destructive. Is there someone you could stop comparing yourself to today?

I am not what I've done or been through; I am what I've conquered and overcome.

Don't let what has happened in your past affect how you approach things in your future. The fact is, pain builds resilience, patience and empathy in us. There's no space for shame in your life. How can you celebrate the person your past has turned you into today?

If you can't change it, change the way you think about it.

Maya Angelou

(Wouldn't Take Nothing for My Journey Now, Random House, 1992)

We can try to focus on the good things in our lives and be genuinely grateful for them but, unfortunately, it won't stop bad things from happening. There will always be aspects of our lives or circumstances that we wish we could change but we just can't. In those times, I have to remind myself that some situations are just out of my control. Then I have to decide how I'm going to view that situation, trusting that things will unfold how they are meant to and I am growing as a consequence.

How can you choose to view a tricky situation you are facing today?

I will not focus on pleasing others.

Something I've learnt over the years is that if you set your life up to please your parents or to appease a romantic partner, it's only you who suffers. I've found that it can be so easy to lose a sense of your own identity if you put what pleases others before what pleases you. It's far better to focus on what brings you joy, peace and hope for the future! What things in your life are a source of joy and contentment for you today?

Be careful when saying things to others that you wouldn't want everyone to hear you say.

My agent always warns me not to say something that I wouldn't want to be a headline on the cover of a newspaper! When I want to say something out of anger or frustration, I ask myself if it represents me well enough to be in print. Sometimes the answer is no, so I have to hold my tongue! It's a really good litmus test for how we speak to others, both online and in person. Often those who post nasty comments online or say mean things behind people's backs aren't terrible people; they've just got caught up in the moment. But words hurt. They can hurt people and reputations. How can you make sure you only say things you're proud of?

I will pursue something that gives me fulfilment.

I love to work hard and it's obviously important for me and my family that I am paid for that work, but I get so much more from my job than money. I find the voluntary work I do with my charitable foundation so fulfilling that I would never give it up. I know some of us don't have the luxury of combining our job with our passion, but it is important that we feel fulfilled.

Maybe for you that could mean a career change in the future, volunteering with a charity or even simply taking up a new creative hobby! What small change could you make to feel more fulfilled in your day-to-day actions exactly where you are?

Every new beginning is an old new beginning's ending.

All things are so intertwined but, rather than feeling held back by that, I find it liberating! It's the circle of life. There's no need to get down about the endings, because they signal new beginnings. It's also important to remember that each new beginning will end at some point. I find great peace in accepting that idea. Can you reframe one ending in your life as a new beginning?

I will breathe.

We hear about this all the time today, and it took me a while to jump on the deep-breathing bandwagon, but I now find meditation to be such a valuable tool. Simply taking time to breathe in and out slowly gives me a sense of calm. When things get a bit much today, could you spare a moment to take a deep breath in and out? Better yet, could you try to find five minutes of quiet to focus on your breathing?

Doubt kills more dreams than failure ever will.

Suzy Kassem

(*Rise Up and Salute the Sun*, Awakened Press, 2011)

You may or may not fail when you try something new – that's a fact of life. In reality, failure isn't scary; it helps us grow. Failing doesn't have to kill a dream; it may just help you refine it so that you can come at it from a different angle. What is just as important as not worrying about failing? Not doubting yourself. I know that failure is possible, but I don't doubt that I can cope with it if it comes and can build something even better after the experience. Can you think of a time when you have 'failed' and come back stronger?

I will choose to engage with content and company that fulfils me.

I try really hard not to endlessly scroll through social media feeds or entertain mindless gossip, but when I slip up and find myself doing this (which I definitely do from time to time), I can feel myself getting irritable and fed up. What I've realized is, when I engage in things that aren't real and don't fulfil me, it lowers my mood and makes me feel that I have no direction. Better to focus on what's real and important to me, like the people I care about! What truly important things can you focus on today?

I won't be suspicious of kindness.

Sometimes someone will do something really nice for me out of the blue. It could be as small as holding a door open for me or giving me their seat on the Tube. I don't know about you, but when people are kind for no reason, I sometimes ask myself, 'Why are they doing that? What do they want?' What I've learnt is that there actually are people who are that kind! When I stop being suspicious, that thought is so comforting. How can you challenge yourself to be a kinder person today?

The greatest challenge in life is discovering who you are. The second greatest is being happy with what you find.

When I was younger, I definitely thought that I knew who I was. Now that I've had a few more years of working things out, I realize that, back then, I knew nothing! I'm sure that in twenty years' time I'll look back at me now and feel the same way. Life is a daily opportunity to learn more about ourselves but, alongside that, we need to learn to love ourselves as we are. Having grace for yourself and your flaws is often the place to start. We're never going to be perfect, but we are doing our best and we are worthy of love. What so-called flaw or imperfection in your life can you embrace this season?

A relationship is a luxury in my life, not a necessity.

When I was single, I was so independent that when I met my husband he was a luxury, not a necessity. I knew that I didn't need a guy to complete me – I was even looking into having a child by adoption or sperm donation, as I didn't have a partner. Taking responsibility for myself was empowering for me and helped me to appreciate a relationship when it came, but I didn't have to rely on it. Is there anything you're longing for that you feel is a necessity, but would actually be a luxury?

I will respect myself by ensuring that others respect my boundaries.

I know that sometimes we can feel we owe people things – our time, our attention or our friendship. The problem is, this can lead us to sacrifice our own needs in favour of the needs of others. It's so important to establish boundaries and to enforce them. You won't be able to be a great friend to those around you if your mental health is suffering because you've taken on too much. How can you make sure you're looking after yourself so that in turn you can help look after others?

Feeling gratitude and not expressing it is like wrapping a present and not giving it.

William Arthur Ward

Gratitude can be so moving that we often feel we have to communicate it to the person who sparked it. There are times, though, when something stops us. We can worry that people will think we're being silly or overly emotional in expressing our heartfelt thanks, but we need to. If we don't, it's like caring for somebody and never telling them. I always think that gratitude is there to be shared. Is it really gratitude if you never express it?

I will never regret being kind.

I think the thing that holds a lot of people back from apologizing or showing someone an act of kindness is worry about how they'll respond, but it's not what they do in return that matters. If you know that you've behaved well, you can hold your head up high. You will never look back and say that you wish you were rude to that person, but you're definitely likely to regret it in the other direction. Kindness is an approach you can always trust. How can you show more kindness today?

Become so confident in who you are that no one's opinion, rejection or behaviour can rock you.

I've had to work really hard to make sure that my confidence levels aren't related to how accepted I feel by others. It's tough to stop other people's opinions swaying how I feel about myself, but it's been such a valuable thing for me to invest in. Ideally, we all want to be unshakable and completely immune to outside influence. In reality, it's not that simple, but we can at least be working towards a strong sense of self that will not be moved off track by other people's storms. Is somebody else's opinion bothering you at the moment? Can you take a deep breath in and out and let that niggle go?

Confidence is silent.
Insecurities are loud.

I think a lot of us assume that the loudest person in the room is the most confident, but when you scratch beneath the surface, often those people are the most fragile and insecure. It's easy for people to feel that if they're brash and loud, they're protected and they can use that behaviour as a wall. If you're a person who does that from time to time, please know that you're enough and you don't need to perform. If you find yourself feeling frustrated with the loud, 'confident' people, can you challenge yourself to remember that all may not be as it seems?

Do what is right, not what is easy.

Roy T. Bennett

(*The Light in the Heart*, self-published, 2020)

Ultimately, I have to ask myself, 'Do you want to have things you want or do you want to be a person of integrity?' I would like to have a quiet life, but sometimes that's the easy route and facing a problem head on is the right thing to do. We have choices to make every single day and I am a great believer in sticking to your morals for each one. Is there a decision you need to make today between the easy route and the right one? Stand strong for what you believe in!

Day 69

I have permission to think that I am good enough.

Sometimes it's more comfortable to put ourselves down than risk looking big-headed. I know a lot of people find it easier to point out their flaws than to highlight their great attributes, but I think that low self-esteem has to be challenged! It's not showing off or self-promoting to say, 'You know what? I am good enough.' You can and should be your biggest cheerleader! What can you give yourself a pat on the back for this week?

I am not stupid if I get something wrong.

I get so frustrated when people feel stupid or, worse, are made to feel stupid for getting something wrong. I get things wrong all the time. We all do! It's how we learn. When I get something wrong, that's when I push myself to develop the most, so how can that be stupid?! Is there something you feel stupid for right now? How can you reframe that thought in a way that demonstrates more self-compassion?

I will choose community over competition.

Over the years I've found that doing things in community with others is often the best way forward. My experience has shown me that it's a far more contented and fulfilled path than each person selfishly pursuing their own gains. You'll find that your progress will be limited if you go it alone anyway. The fact is, we can get much further and achieve much more as a group. What could you invite other people into today?

I will love fearlessly today.

I believe that to love fearlessly is to be truly honest and vulnerable about how you feel. There is great risk in giving love so freely and it's important to remember that love and pain often go hand in hand. Even when you love the right person, there will be upsets and disappointment along the way, but don't let that stop you from loving with all your heart. The reward is always worth the risk, even if it doesn't look how you first imagined it. Can you think of or imagine a time in which the risk will be worth it?

Those who follow the crowd usually get lost in it.

Rick Warren

(*The Purpose Driven Life*, Zondervan, 2009)

At different times in my life, I've both followed the crowd and decided to follow my own path. Not being able to blend in with the masses has turned out to be one of my biggest strengths. It took some time, but now I am able to do my own thing and make the decision that feels right for me – not for everybody else. Is there an area of your life where you need to step out?

Crying can bring relief, as long as you don't cry alone.

Anne Frank

It's important to know that crying doesn't mean you're failing to cope. It's not shameful to cry – in fact, it can be cathartic. If you can, reach out to a friend so you have someone to talk to about you how you're feeling. Is there anyone you could invite to support you while you cry?

Be careful when you follow the masses. Sometimes the 'm' is silent.

I love a cheeky affirmation to mix things up! We can all get swept up in the energy of a crowd without stopping to ask ourselves if we actually want to be there. It happens all too easily, but the consequences can be disastrous. We can avoid mob mentality, though, by taking a step back and a deep breath and each asking ourselves, 'Do I really want to be a part of this?'

There are far, far better things ahead than any we leave behind.

C. S. Lewis

(Letter to Mary Willis Shelburne, 17 June 1963, in C. S. Lewis, *Letters to an American Lady*, Wm. B. Eerdmans, [1963] 2014. Copyright UK CS Lewis Pte Ltd 1963; USA Wm. B. Eerdmans, [1963] 2014. Reprinted with permission.)

I know that everyone has a past. I also know that it's totally normal to reflect on your past, especially if you don't feel able to move on yet. When I start to feel down about things that happened long ago, I find it's important to remember that whatever is in the future, it will be better and greater than before. As a person of faith, I trust that what God has in store for me is what is right, and I won't regret it! What can you put your trust in today?

Fall in love with somebody who will never let you go to sleep wondering if you still matter.

Particularly when I was younger, I used to fall into the trap of going for the guy who kept me on my toes. As I've got older, I've realized that to cause uncertainty in someone isn't a sign of attraction; it's just plain being mean. If someone doesn't realize your value and show it through consistent love, care and attention, then perhaps that person isn't the right one for you to have in your life. Is there someone who keeps you on your toes but should actually be holding you steady?

Sometimes the worst place you can be is in your own head.

Our minds are powerful; they can be our biggest creator but also our biggest torturer. When it feels as if my thoughts are running away with me, that's when I call on my friends to help me out. The fact that we can be our own worst enemy is why we need those real connections in our lives. My friends will often help me to rationalize the thoughts that are causing me distress and encourage me to find healthy ways to decompress. What healthy action could you take to relieve some of the stress in your head? Maybe today is the day to set aside an hour for walking, exercise or a hobby or craft?

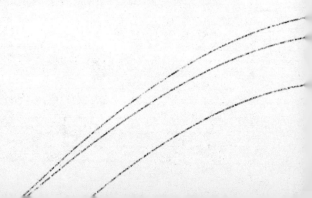

We're products of our past but we don't have to be prisoners of it.

Rick Warren

I once had a counsellor who said to me, 'Trauma is inevitable but it doesn't have to be a life sentence.' I've thought a lot about that since and the more I think about it, the truer it feels. Ultimately, though, nothing external is going to set you free; it's your mindset or making the brave decision to put your trust in something bigger than you entirely. How is your mindset today? Can you take five minutes to be still and let your mind refocus on the day ahead of you?

Today, I will focus on one thing at a time.

Anyone who has gone through any kind of recovery that takes a long time will know this is key to that journey. There's no point projecting forwards. It helps us to keep going if we just focus on the day we are in and face the trials that come with it. Each day is substantial and really important. What might help you keep your focus in the present today?

I don't have to be cheerful all the time. I will not be afraid to show people my uncomfortable side.

We can't always feel our best, physically or mentally, but I've learnt that I don't need to put on a brave face for everyone. Don't be scared to show people who you really are, and how you really feel. You don't need to be constantly upbeat and happy. In fact, others may feel closer to you when they see how real and vulnerable you can be. Who might you be able to be vulnerable with this week?

I will see the value in collaboration.

We may often feel we can't be bothered to get other people involved in our projects – or even our lives! I know I've felt that there's no point sometimes, because those people may let me down or hurt me. What I've learnt in the past few years, though, is that there really is strength in numbers and when you allow people into your project or vision and collaborate with them, it is powerful. Can you see an area in your life which could benefit from some collaboration?

I can't control everything that happens, but I can control how I respond.

I don't agree with the classic saying 'Life is what you make it'. Some things are out of your control and others happen to you that you couldn't have influenced with positivity or by changing your behaviour. Knowing that you can control some things and identifying those in difficult moments, though, can be immensely helpful. In the end, you are in control of how you respond to trials, how you store up negative things and how long you allow them to live, rent-free, in your mind. What stressful situation or complex circumstance can you relinquish control of today?

I haven't failed.
I have learnt.

For me, the idea that 'nothing is a failure, just a rehearsal' is one that takes a while to sink in. I have to say it out loud over and over! The truth is, though, when we realize that our 'failures' help us to develop into the people we want to be and grow the skills we need, we will stop resenting them and embrace them. What failure of yours, or even another's, can you embrace this week?

I will be willing to be a beginner every single morning.

Meister Eckhart

It's OK to be new. Everyone had to begin somewhere, so you shouldn't feel embarrassed or upset when you have to start from scratch. What I think is most impressive is when people persevere. You won't be a beginner for ever and just imagine how great it will feel when, after some hard work, it clicks into place for you! Can you recall a time when you went from being a beginner at something to finally having that thing 'click' for you?

I will focus on the best elements of my day.

When I sit down at the end of the day to think about how it went, I always try to focus on the best parts. I know that we need to acknowledge the bad, but so often we *only* acknowledge the bad. We need to start telling ourselves a different story, to focus on the time spent with loved ones, the uplifting conversations and all those glorious small wins! Can you recall three things you are thankful for today?

I will inhale love and exhale hate.

Filling yourself with love and actively choosing to breathe it into your body will help you to develop empathy for those around you. There's no need to bring hate into your mind and body. If I ever do allow it to creep in, I just remember that there's no need to keep it there! What would it feel like to just breathe in love and compassion, and breathe out the negative bits?

I won't let a bad day become a bad week, month or year.

We all have bad days when things don't go our way and we're disappointed by the outcome. I've found that it's so important not to allow those disappointments to spill over into other aspects of my life and ruin not only that moment but also that day, week or month. I try to stop negative incidents taking more space in my life than they need to. Is there a negative incident that you need to let go of today?

Opportunities are everywhere.
I just need to choose to see them.

We all have a friend who loves a good moan. On the wrong day, that friend could be me! I've found that having the right attitude is really important. If you can, get into the mindset that nothing is set in stone and you can change things at any time – you will find you feel freer. Opportunity is everywhere if you're open to seeing it. Can you make a mental note every time you recognize a new opportunity today?

It's OK for someone to let me down. I'm strong enough to cope with it.

I have to remind myself regularly that I am far stronger than I realize. Being let down is inevitable, but we all have an inner strength to withstand it, whether we know it or not! You've built an endurance that is greater than you know. When things are really overwhelming, can you take some quiet time to recharge and tap into that inner strength?

I won't focus on being busy, but on being productive.

In society, I find that we glorify being busy too much. There aren't any prizes for rushing round like mad and running ourselves into the ground! Rather than being mindlessly busy, I try to prioritize my time and focus on the things, and especially the people, that mean the most to me. When I am working, I try to make sure that time is used productively so I can relax and enjoy it when I clock off. The same can be true for what we think about. If you find yourself mindlessly ruminating over the same problems, trying to solve them, then perhaps you need to challenge yourself to be more productive in your thinking. Can you set aside fifteen minutes today for your busy mind to try and problem solve and then turn your mind to other things?

I will help others to shine brighter.

I've noticed that a lot of people who have big followings on social media have been handing their accounts to lesser-known people who represent great causes. It allows those people to use their big platforms to shine a light on the issues they believe in. I love seeing people boost others and share their space! I know not everyone has millions of followers or even has access to social media, but there are various ways in which we can help others to shine brightly. Could you tell some friends about someone who is doing great work or say thank you to someone who is doing a great job today?

I will not be afraid of saying the wrong thing.

We are often taught that getting things wrong is shameful. We can be afraid that if we don't manage to express ourselves in the most articulate way, we will sound stupid, and people won't want to listen to us. Sometimes we even sit back and allow others to talk for us, not asserting ourselves because we don't want to make a fuss. It's so important that you know your voice is valuable. Never be afraid to speak out! Is there something you need to say out loud today – to yourself or someone else?

Character cannot be developed in ease and quiet. Only through experience of trial and suffering can the soul be strengthened, ambition inspired and success achieved.

Helen Keller

It's so true that the skills we develop in times of trial can really shape us. The more I think about so-called 'problems', the more I think that we should rename them! Are they 'problems' if they are helping us to grow in such amazing ways? It's through them that we develop into the people we're supposed to be. What 'problems' or trials in your life can you begin to reframe today? Where have you seen 'fruit' from the fight?

I only fail when I stop trying.

Giving up on something feels so final to me. It takes a lot for me to walk away from something I'm passionate about. I always say, 'While I'm alive, I'm still going!' Is there a project or even a person you may have given up on too quickly?

No act of kindness, no matter how small, is ever wasted.

I remember the big, monumental things that people have done for me in my life, but also the small acts of kindness. I mean the really small things, like holding a door open or putting the kettle on. They're so everyday that the people won't even remember doing them! In this way, your impact can be way larger than you realize, because you won't always know how much that tiny thing meant to someone else. Can you recognize some tiny things that you have done today or perhaps you could have done that would have made a big difference?

I can listen and support without having to solve.

Often what's needed in a situation isn't for us to try to fix people and solve problems. While strategizing has its place, what's more important is that people feel heard. It's natural to try to give someone a solution when you see that person hurting, but sometimes it's better simply to acknowledge that things can be tough. Can you lend someone a listening ear today?

I will take the time to look for beauty today.

We can choose to step out of the door in the morning and keep our heads down or we can look up and see wonder all around us. Even when our circumstances mean that we can't get out and about, the same applies; it's often not the scene that changes, it's our perspective. There is so much beauty in the people we see, the moments we enjoy and creation around us. Where can you see beauty today?

Courage doesn't always roar. Sometimes courage is the quiet voice at the end of the day saying (whispering), 'I will try again tomorrow.'

Mary Anne Radmacher

We shouldn't confuse courage with being loud and ballsy. Sometimes it's the people who silently keep going, day after day, through challenge after challenge, who are the bravest of all. When things haven't gone your way, look at the next day and see it as a chance to have another go. What did you try today that you may need to try again tomorrow?

I will continue to believe that the best days are in front of me.

I don't think this necessarily means that every experience you have in the future will be better than the ones you have had in the past, but I do think that, as we get older, we learn how to find a deeper level of joy in things. I also think that we learn more about how difficult life can be, so we get greater enjoyment from the good things that we do experience.

If you're going through a tough time now, remember that the best is yet to come, and this hard place might help you enjoy the days ahead even more. Why not begin this book again or flick back to your favourite affirmations as you step forward into your future with a little bit more hope?

Acknowledgements

My first and biggest thank you goes to you; to every person who has faithfully bought and gifted my books, connected with me and generally cheered me on. I am constantly inspired by the stories I hear and the messages I receive from you. They push me forward to keep writing books like this one. You have all my love and gratitude. Thank you for being an ever-positive presence in my life.

I, of course, also need to offer a big shout-out to those who get the 'not so positive' side of me but lift me up all the same: my best friend – my husband – my supportive family and my children. You are the daily tonic that makes me smile on the darkest of days.

Huge and heartfelt thank yous to my publishing team at SPCK – Elizabeth Neep, Joy Tibbs, Michelle Clark and Sam Snedden – and to Lauren Windle for sharing my vision, believing in me and wanting to spread positivity. Thank you also to the team at Fresh Partners and Belle PR for being as passionate as I am about this project and always supporting me in all I do.

Last, but certainly not least, I want to thank every person who has engaged with my daily affirmations on social media. Sharing those snippets of hope with you throughout the global pandemic and subsequent national lockdowns made me feel so close to you all as we journeyed through such a strange and surreal time together. Many of you said that you wanted me to write a new book of affirmations and here it is – but it's not *my* book, it's *ours*, and I look forward to sharing these affirmations with you over the coming days, weeks and months.

If you enjoyed this book, you may also want to
share a little bit of hope with the little ones in your life
through Katie's debut children's book, *All You Need*.
Adventure with Teeny Mouse through wise words
and delightful illustrations as she learns that all she
needs may be closer than she thinks!

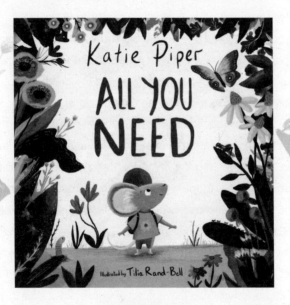

978-0-281-08656-6

spckpublishing.co.uk